The Twelve Days of Christmas

Illustrated by Vladimir Vagin

HARPERCOLLINSPUBLISHERS

The illustrations in this book are watercolor paintings.

The Twelve Days of Christmas   Illustrations copyright © 1999 by Vladimir Vagin
Printed in the U.S.A. All rights reserved.

Library of Congress Cataloging-in-Publication Data
Twelve days of Christmas (English folk song)
    The twelve days of Christmas / illustrated by Vladimir Vagin.
        p.   cm.
    Summary: On each of the twelve days of Christmas, unusual and fanciful gifts arrive to
celebrate the season.
    ISBN 0-06-027652-5. — ISBN 0-06-028399-8 (lib. bdg.)
    1. Folk songs, English—England—Texts.   2. Christmas music—Texts.   [1. Folk
songs—England.   2. Christmas music.]   I. Vagin, Vladimir Vasil 'evich, date, ill.
PZ8.3. T8517   1998   97-11749
782.42'1723'0268   CIP
[E]—dc21   AC

Typography by Al Cetta   1 2 3 4 5 6 7 8 9 10   ❖   First Edition

For Galia

On the first day of Christmas

my true love gave to me

a partridge in a pear tree.

On the second day of Christmas

my true love gave to me

two turtledoves,

and a partridge in a pear tree.

On the third day of Christmas

my true love gave to me

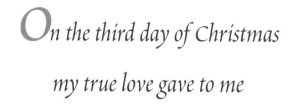

three French hens,

two turtledoves,

and a partridge in a pear tree.

On the fourth day of Christmas

my true love gave to me

four calling birds,

three French hens,

two turtledoves,

and a partridge in a pear tree.

On the fifth day of Christmas

my true love gave to me

five golden rings,

four calling birds,

three French hens,

two turtledoves,

and a partridge in a pear tree.

On the sixth day of Christmas

my true love gave to me

six geese a-laying,

five golden rings,

four calling birds,

three French hens,

two turtledoves,

and a partridge in a pear tree.

On the seventh day of Christmas

my true love gave to me

seven swans a-swimming,

six geese a-laying,

five golden rings,

four calling birds,

three French hens,

two turtledoves,

and a partridge in a pear tree.

On the eighth day of Christmas

my true love gave to me

eight maids a-milking,

seven swans a-swimming,

six geese a-laying,

five golden rings,

four calling birds,

three French hens,

two turtledoves,

and a partridge in a pear tree.

On the ninth day of Christmas

my true love gave to me

nine ladies dancing,

eight maids a-milking,

seven swans a-swimming,

six geese a-laying,

five golden rings,

four calling birds,

three French hens,

two turtledoves,

and a partridge in a pear tree.

CROSS SCHOOL LIBRARY

On the tenth day of Christmas

my true love gave to me

ten lords a-leaping

nine ladies dancing,

eight maids a-milking,

seven swans a-swimming,

six geese a-laying,

five golden rings,

four calling birds,

three French hens,

two turtledoves,

and a partridge in a pear tree.

On the eleventh day of Christmas

my true love gave to me

eleven pipers piping,

ten lords a-leaping,

nine ladies dancing,

eight maids a-milking,

seven swans a-swimming,

six geese a-laying,

five golden rings,

four calling birds,

three French hens,

two turtledoves,

and a partridge in a pear tree.

On the twelfth day of Christmas

my true love gave to me

twelve drummers drumming,

eleven pipers piping,

ten lords a-leaping,

nine ladies dancing,

eight maids a-milking,

seven swans a-swimming,

six geese a-laying,

five golden rings,

four calling birds,

three French hens,

two turtledoves,

and a partridge in a pear tree.

The Twelve Days of Christmas

On the first day of Christ-mas my true love gave to me a par-tridge in a pear tree. On the

sec-ond day of Christ-mas my true love gave to me two tur-tle-doves, and a par-tridge in a pear tree. On the third day of Christ-mas my

true love gave to me three French hens, two tur-tle-doves, and a par-tridge in a pear tree. On the fourth day of Christ-mas my

true love gave to me four call-ing birds, three French hens, two tur-tle-doves, and a par-tridge in a pear tree. On the

fifth day of Christ-mas my true love gave to me five gold-en rings, four call-ing birds, three French hens,

two tur-tle-doves, and a par-tridge in a pear tree. On the sixth day of Christ-mas my true love gave to me six geese a-lay-ing,
seventh   seven swans a-swim-ming,
eighth   eight maids a-milk-ing,
ninth   nine la-dies danc-ing,
tenth   ten lords a-leap-ing,
eleventh   eleven pip-ers pip-ing,
twelfth   twelve drum-mers drum-ming,

five gold-en rings, four call-ing birds, three French hens, two tur-tle-doves and a par-tridge in a pear tree.

On the twelfth day of Christmas

my true love gave to me

twelve drummers drumming,

eleven pipers piping,

ten lords a-leaping,

nine ladies dancing,

eight maids a-milking,

seven swans a-swimming,

six geese a-laying,

five golden rings,

four calling birds,

three French hens,

two turtledoves,

and a partridge in a pear tree.

About the Twelve Days of Christmas

People began celebrating the Twelve Days of Christmas—the days between Christmas and Epiphany on January 6—more than a thousand years ago. No one knows exactly when the music and words for the song "The Twelve Days of Christmas" were created, but some say they date from the Middle Ages, when the "counting song" form was popular. The song was first published in England in 1780, at which time it grew in popularity among both children and adults.

The Christmas holiday has historically been a lavish affair, with twelve days set aside for gift giving, feasting, and merrymaking. Benevolent landowners used the holiday as a way to provide their tenants with a respite from the cold and dreary winter. At least once during the twelve-day season, peasants went to the manor house for food, drink, dancing, and games, including, on the last night, a recitation of "The Twelve Days of Christmas." Originally this recitation was a kind of game, in which the first participant recited the first line, the second recited the second and first lines, and so on. Each additional line meant recalling all those that preceded it, and woe to the hapless player with a poor memory. Missing a single line meant he or she had to give a gift to the group.

The Christmas season has evolved and changed with the times, as have the words of "The Twelve Days of Christmas." "Calling birds" were originally "colly birds," a term for blackbirds; "golden rings" may have been "goldspinks," meaning goldfinches. But colly birds or calling birds, twelve days or fewer, Christmas—and its spirit of joy, giving, and love—remains the same.

#7379

ワ379

ワ379

E
782.42
TWE

001426569

The twelve days of
Christmas

$15.89

DATE DUE	BORROWER'S NAME	ROOM NO.
9/14	Miguel	LCD
JAN 7 '02	Jerome	3H
11-6	Glen	1C
11-15	Glen	1C
NOV 26 '02	Stephanie	2D

001426569

E
782.42
TWE

The twelve days of
Christmas

WENDELL CROSS LIBRARY
WATERBURY, CT   06706

381790 01589   329658   007